THE DEADLIEST DISEASES IN HISTORY

BIOLOGY FOR KIDS

Children's Biology Books

BABY PROFESSOR
EDUCATION KIDS

Speedy Publishing LLC
40 E. Main St. #1156
Newark, DE 19711
www.speedypublishing.com

Everybody gets sick sometimes. But sometimes, a lot of people get sick at the same time. This is called an epidemic or a pandemic. Read on and find out about the most dangerous diseases that cause epidemics, and what they have done to people.

HERE COME INFECTIOUS DISEASES

White blood cells flowing through red blood as a microbiology symbol of the human immune system fighting off infections.

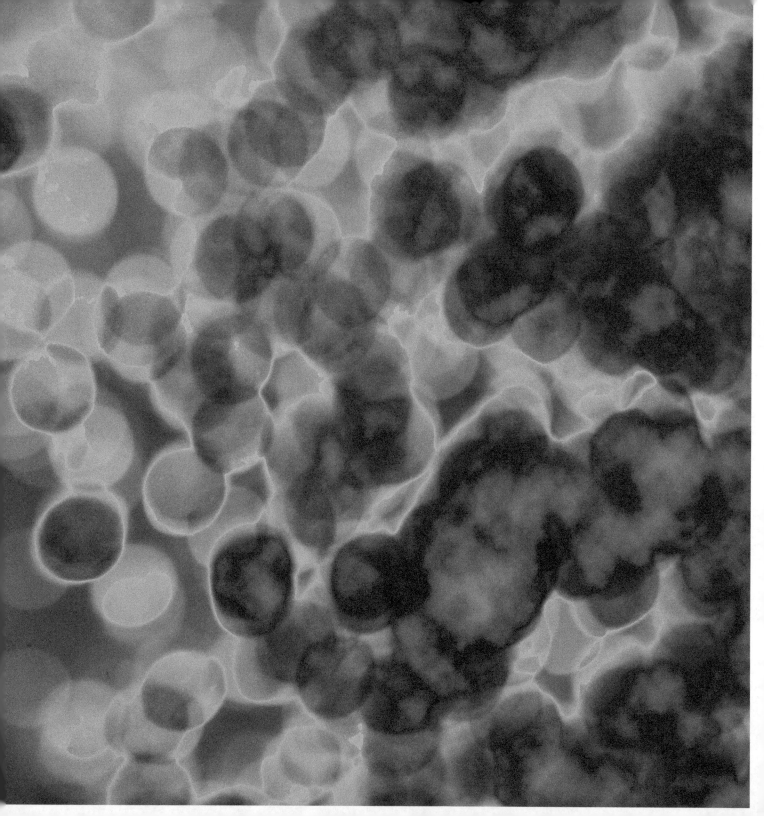

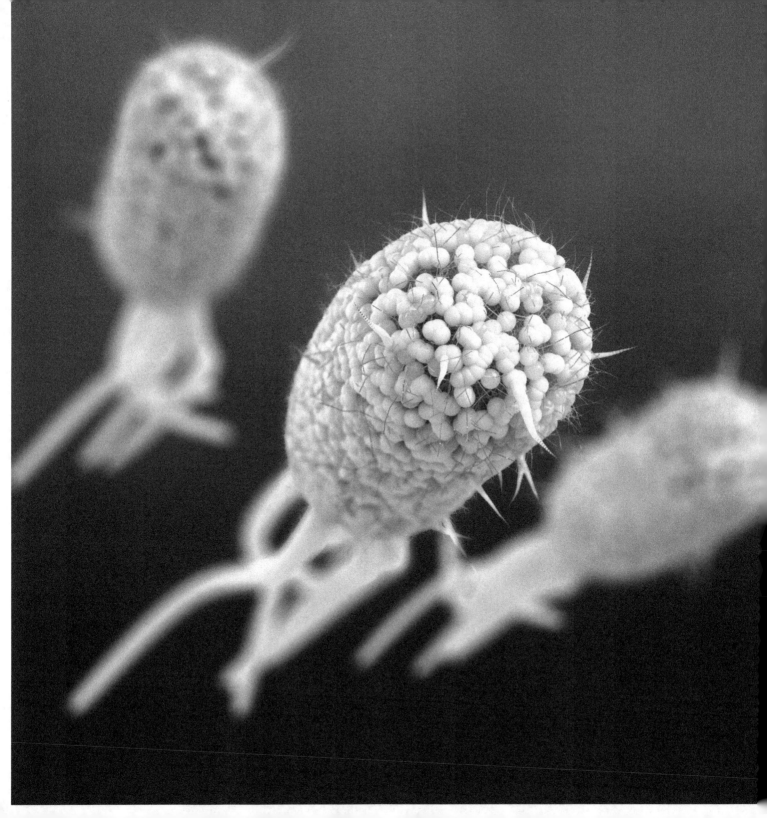

Bacteria, fungi, viruses and parasites are the main creators and carriers of infectious diseases. Not all bacteria are always bad, and in fact some live in our body all the time. But when bad bacteria or other disease-carriers start getting passed around, they can make a lot of people sick, or even die, very quickly.

Escherichia Coli (E. Coli.)

Sometimes infectious diseases pass from animals to people, or through insect bites. Sometimes we eat food that is contaminated, or drink water that has parasites. Sometimes a sick person sneezes on us, or we touch something they have touched. Then, in a few days, we may be sick, even seriously sick, ourselves.

Ill woman sneezing into a tissue. Virus floating into the air.

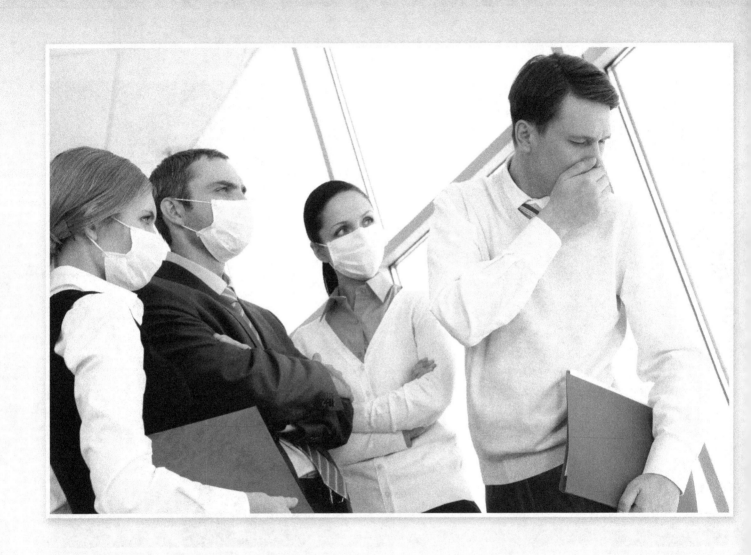

SYMPTOMS

Symptoms vary from disease to disease, but usually they include a high fever and feeling very tired. Sometimes you can get better just by resting and drinking a lot of fluids, but serious infectious diseases call for a serious medical response: doctor visits, medicine, and maybe a trip to the hospital.

Group of associates in protective masks looking strictly at coughing man.

PREVENTION

The spread of many infectious diseases has been slowed, or even prevented, by vaccination. Diseases like measles and chickenpox, that used to be common, are very rare now in countries that practice vaccination.

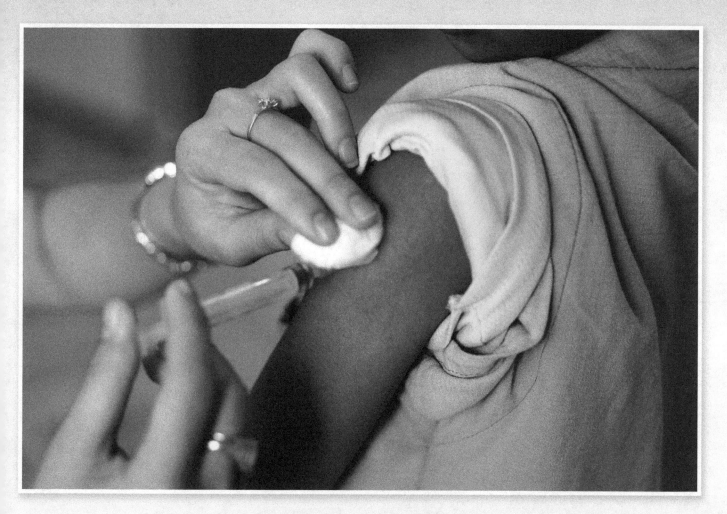

Injection with a syringe to prevent flu.

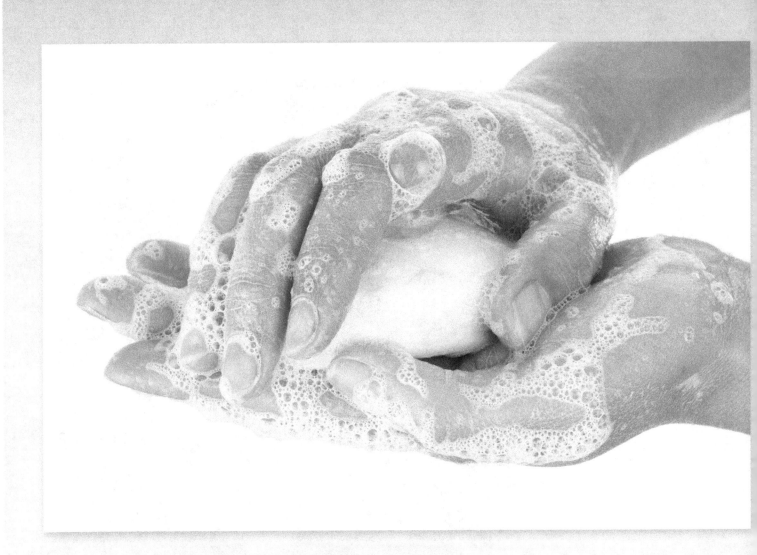

Washing hands.

The most basic day-to-day action you can take to reduce the chance of picking up an infectious disease is washing your hands with soap and water frequently: after going to the bathroom, after coming in from playing, even after holding the handle of a shopping cart or touching a door handle that other people touch. You can't see infection, so you can't know it's not there. If you make hand-washing a habit, you can increase your chances of staying healthy.

SMALLPOX

Variola Virus (Smallpox), a highly contagious and deadly disease.

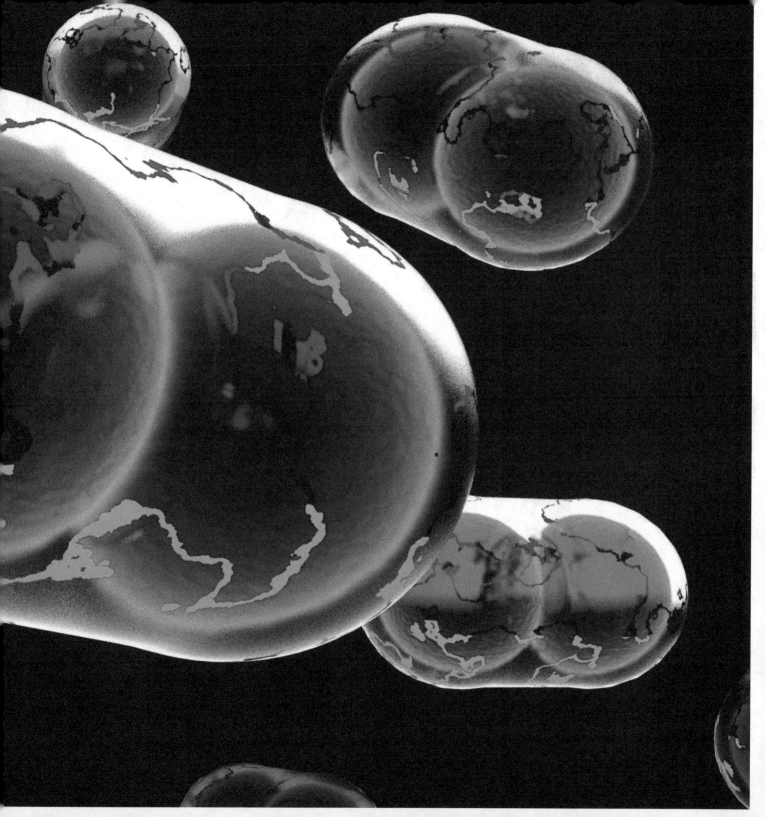

Smallpox was among the most deadly infectious diseases in human history. Just in the twentieth century, smallpox killed as many as 500 million people.

Smallpox has officially been eliminated from the list of threats, but some laboratories keep samples of the virus so they can develop new vaccines if it reappears.

Edward Jenner (1749- 1823), Physician and pioneer of vaccination, vaccinating 8 year old James Phipps with cowpox to provide immunity against smallpox, 1796.

One of the strangest threats of climate change is that, as frozen areas of tundra are warming, they may release long-dormant strands of smallpox, among other diseases. Learn more about changes to our planet in the Baby Professor book *Mother Earth Needs a Band-Aid!*

Tabular Iceberg and Brash Ice, Antarctica.

Smallpox wiped out the vast majority of the Native American populations of North, Central, and South America. Millions of people died after early European explorers or invaders brought the disease. Squanto, a Pawtuxet living in what is now Massachusetts, was

kidnapped and taken to England in 1615. He left a vibrant community of thousands of people. When he returned in 1619, smallpox had ravaged the tribes of the eastern coast of North America. Where there had been lively villages, Squanto found only bones.

When the Spanish invaded Mexico, one soldier was sick with smallpox and died. He passed his illness on to the Aztecs, and the infection destroyed almost their entire army.

So far, smallpox is the only infectious disease affecting humans that we have managed to wipe out completely.

Smallpox was introduced into Mexico by the Spanish expedition of Panfilo de Narvaez and raged through the Aztec capital Tenochtitlan in late 1520.

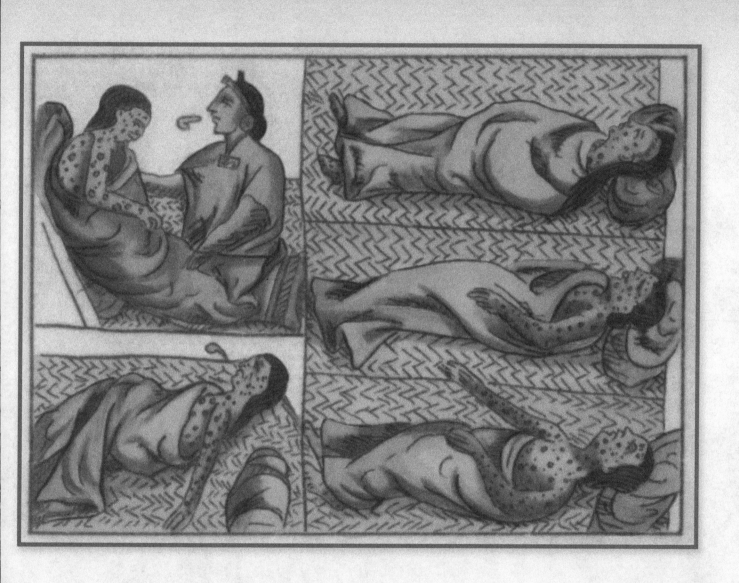

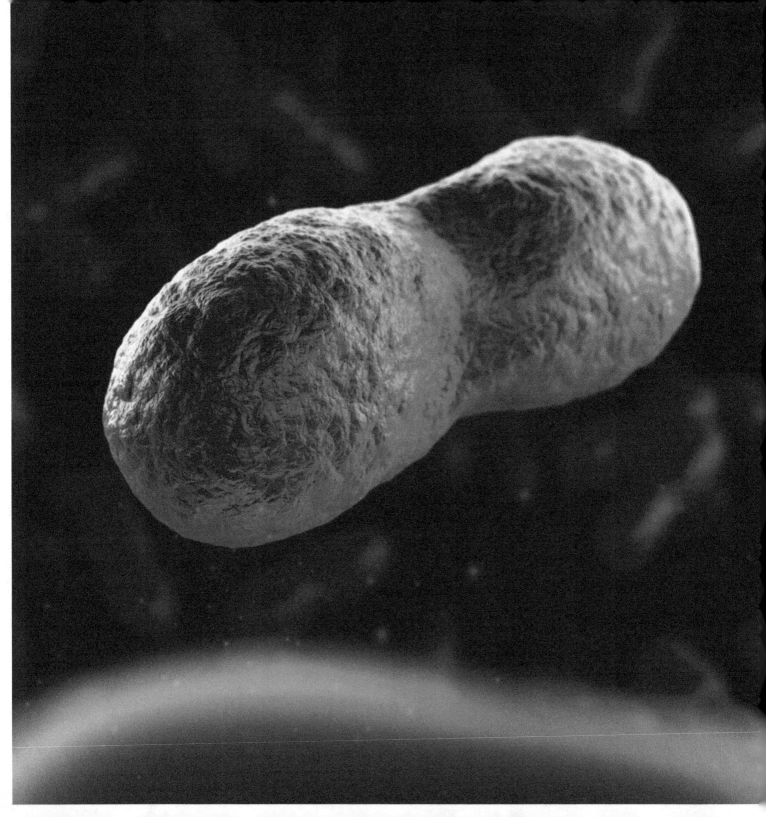

BUBONIC PLAGUE

The bubonic plague is also known as the Black Death. It periodically caused thousands of deaths across Asia, the Near East, and Europe. Between 1348 and 1350, the plague killed one person out of every three in Europe, devastating societies.

Bubonic plague bacteria, Yersinia pestis.

Bubonic plague is a bacterial infection. Its name comes from the **"*buboes*"**, or swellings, that appear on the skin. Once a person catches the disease, he may be dead within hours. Fortunately, modern antibiotics can hold off the bacterium, Yersinia pestis.

Outbreaks still happen, however. Usually people get bubonic plague after they have been bitten by fleas that had already bitten an animal, usually a rat, that was itself sick with the disease.

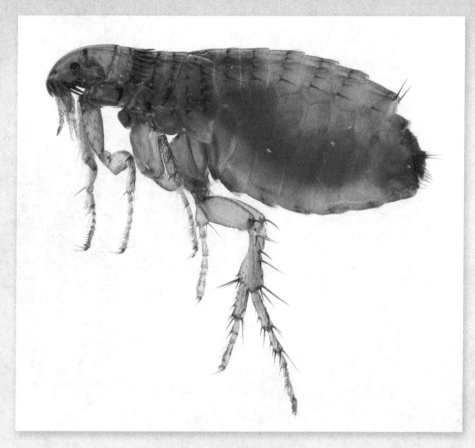

Flea

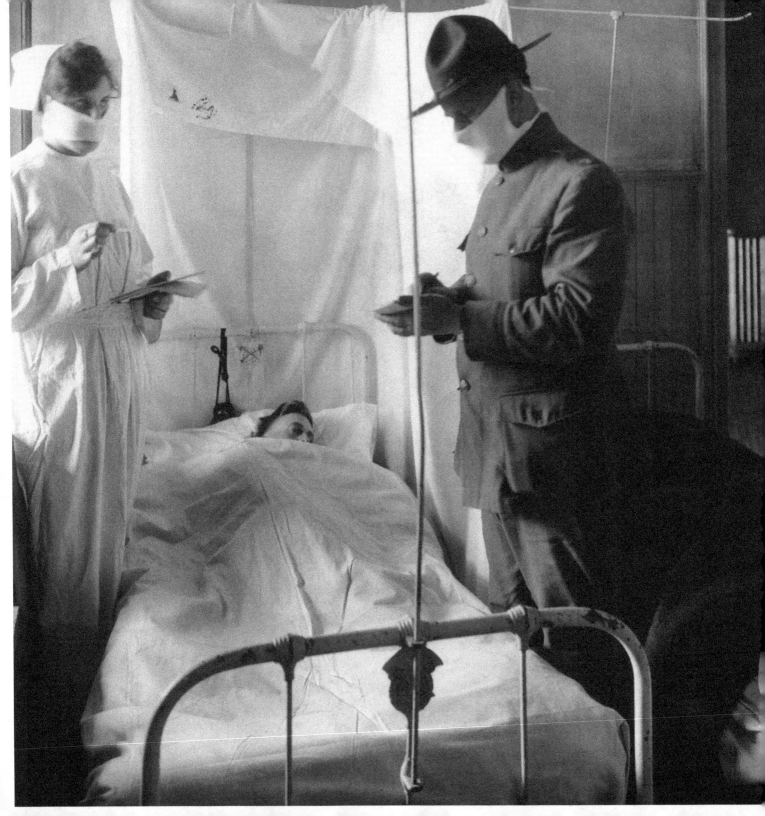

SPANISH FLU

At the end of World War I, the Spanish flu caused illness and death around the world. In North America, it was made worse by the return of troops from the war. At each stop across Canada, for instance, troop trains dropped off soldiers returning home, and they brought the Spanish flu with them.

Spanish Influenza in American Army hospitals.

World War I caused the deaths of at least 18 million people, mainly soldiers. The Spanish flu caused the deaths of up to 50 million people around the world—men, women, and children.

The cause of the Spanish flu was the H1N1 influenza virus. This same virus caused another epidemic in 2009, swine flu. Fortunately modern medicine was able to deal with this outbreak.

Soldiers gargle with salt and water to prevent influenza, during the 1918-19 'Spanish' Influenza pandemic. Camp Dix, New Jersey. Sept. 24, 1918.

Serbian epidemic.of typhus fever. 1920.

TYPHUS

Typhus is caused by a bacterial infection spread by body lice, fleas and chiggers. The symptoms include fever, a rash, and a headache. Epidemics of typhus usually take place in crowded conditions with poor sanitation and little access to clean water.

There is no vaccine generally available to prevent typhus. The way to reduce its spread it is to reduce the insects and conditions that let it me transmitted from person to person.

People wrote about typhus as early as 1528. Its name is from the Greek word that describes an unclear mind. That's the experience of people suffering from typhus!

Fever, represented as a frenzied beast, stands racked in the centre of a room, while a blue monster, representing ague, ensnares his victim by the fireside; a doctor writes prescriptions to the right, by T. Rowlandson, 1788.

Designed by James Dunthorne.   Etchd by T. Rowlandson.

And feel by turns the bitter change of fierce extremes,   AGUE & FEVER.   _extremes by change more fierce._

Milton.

Pub. as the Act directs March 29 1788 by T. Rowlandson. N.º 50 Poland Street.

TYPHOID FEVER

Typhoid fever is a different nasty infection from typhus. It is a bacterial infection related to Salmonella. It causes a high fever, weakness, stomach pain, and headaches. People who are already weakened for some other reason may be in severe danger from typhoid fever.

The habitat of cockroaches as based Waste roaches, lead to many diseases transmitted to humans, such as diarrhea, dysentery, typhoid, cholera, or food poisoning.

People catch typhoid fever by drinking or eating contaminated water or food. Outbreaks happen where sanitation is not good.

Typhoid fever caused many deaths in the past, and still does in underdeveloped parts of the world. Fortunately, there is now a vaccine to prevent catching the disease, as well as effective treatments should you fall ill with it.

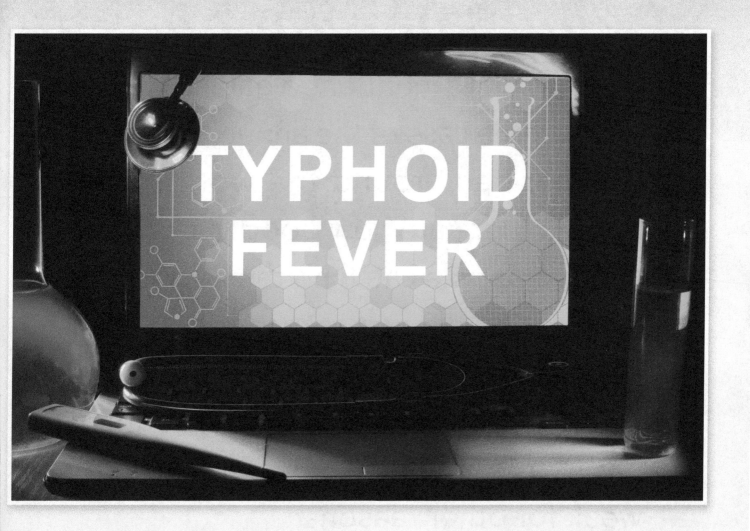

SEASONAL FLU

Spanish flu, mentioned earlier, was an extreme case of the annual flu events that happen around the world. Even though there are now good vaccines to prevent people catching the flu, millions fall ill every year and as many as 500,000 people die. Those most likely to die are the elderly, the very young, pregnant women, and those who are already weak for other reasons.

Sick couple with the flu.

Healthy people usually recover in a few days if they rest and take plenty of fluids.

TUBERCULOSIS

Tuberculosis is caused by a bacterium that is evolving to become more and more resistant to treatment. Tuberculosis has been a global experience in the past, and still causes the deaths of over 1.5 million people each year, mainly in developing countries.

Tuberculosis affects the lungs, and it is spread when an infected person coughs, sneezes, or talks near others.

Pulmonary tuberculosis.

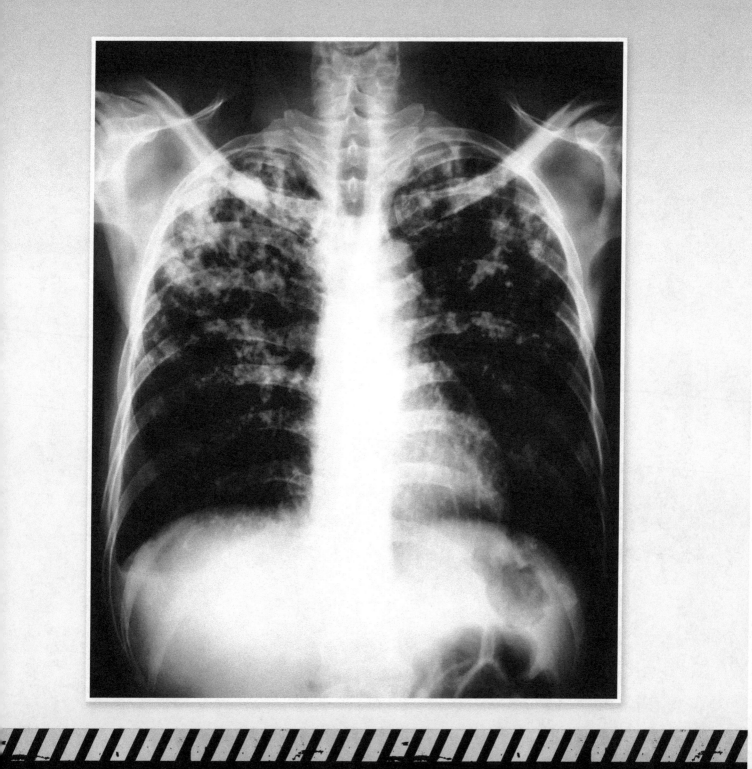

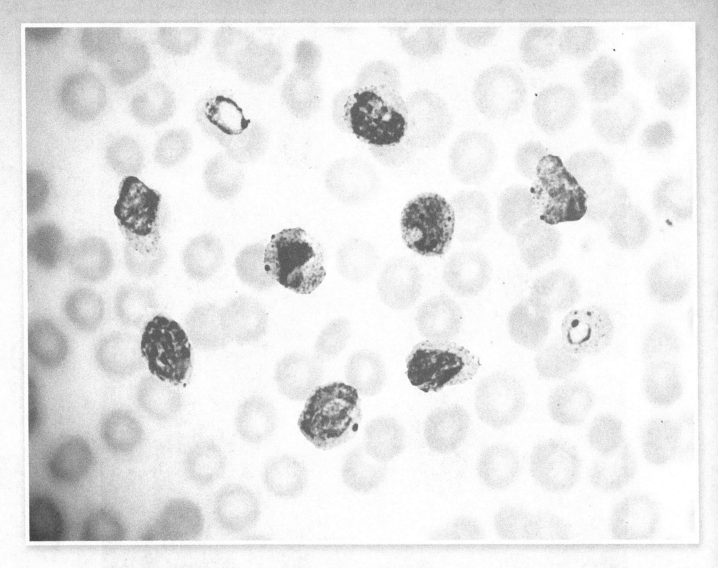

Malaria parasite.

MALARIA

A parasite causes malaria, and over a million people die of this disease every year. An infected mosquito can give a person malaria with a bite, and the infection often kills small children.

Most people get malaria in tropical parts of the world, but as global warming raises temperatures everywhere, there are fears that the range of malaria may spread.

Read more about global warming in the Baby Professor book *What Every Child Should Know about Climate Change.*

There is no malaria vaccine at this time, and treatments are not always effective.

Mosquito

Close-up of African Child drinking water.

CHOLERA

Cholera is a bacterial disease. People catch it when they drink water contaminated with the bacteria. It used to kill hundreds of thousands of people in epidemics, and still kills over 100,000 people a year in parts of the world where it is hard to get clean drinking water. People can die within hours if they do not get treatment.

The first great cholera outbreak was in India from 1817 to 1823. Nobody knows how many civilians died during this epidemic, but 10,000 British soldiers were among the dead.

Cholera traveled to other countries in contaminated water in sailing ships, or when people who were already infected brought the disease with them.

Copenhagen cholera outbreak, 1853.

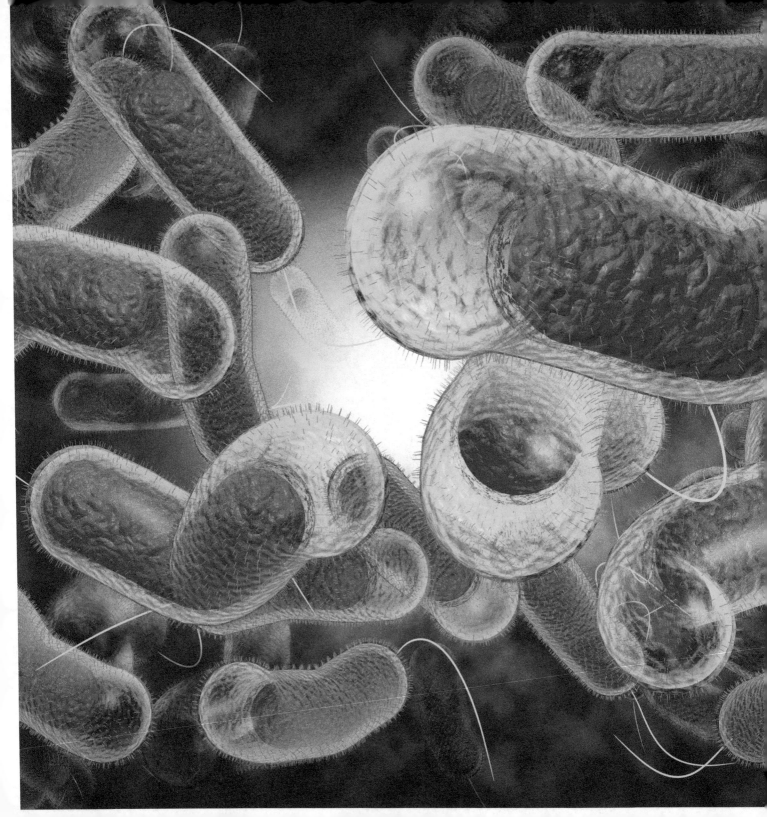

There have been seven major cholera epidemics since 1817. Fighting it has led to great advances in sanitation and providing clean water in cities, but the disease is still very dangerous. In the 1947 cholera epidemic in Egypt, 30,000 people fell ill with the disease. Of them, 20,000 died!

Cholera Bacteria.

HIV/AIDS

AIDS, or autoimmune deficiency syndrome, is caused by a virus for which, so far, there is no preventative vaccine. Since 1981, when it was discovered, AIDS has killed over 25 million people around the world.

There is no cure for AIDS so far, but treatments have been developed that have helped reduce its death rate. Many people live long and productive lives even after being diagnosed as HIV positive.

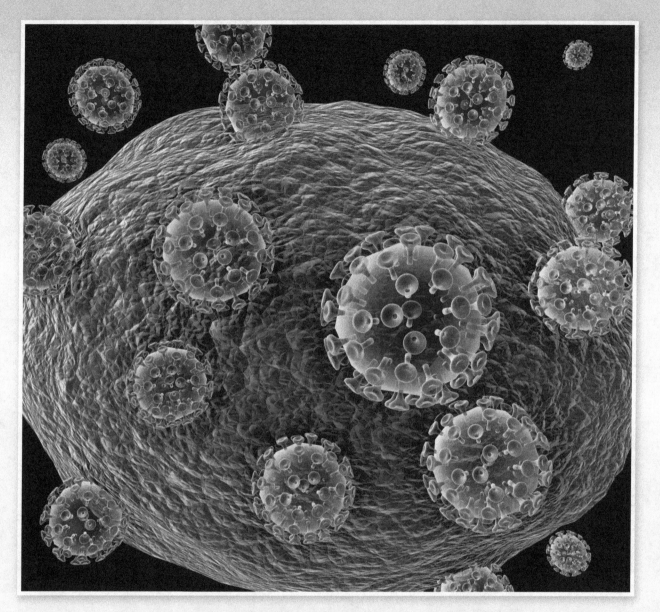

HIV Viruses Attacking Cell.

Woman making heart shape in front of
AIDS awareness ribbon.

In developing countries, the death rate is still very high. Almost 30 million people in Africa south of the Sahara Desert are living with AIDS, with little access to treatment.

AIDS is generally transmitted by unprotected sex or the use of dirty hypodermic needles.

KEEP HEALTHY!

Y ou can do a lot to keep yourself safe from these dangerous diseases, and even from less-scary illnesses like the common cold. See the Baby Professor book ***Germ Smart! Infectious Diseases for Kids*** to learn more about keeping free of infectious diseases.

Using cleaning spray to kill germs.

Visit

BABY PROFESSOR
EDUCATION KIDS

www.BabyProfessorBooks.com

to download Free Baby Professor eBooks
and view our catalog of new and exciting
Children's Books

CPSIA information can be obtained
at www.ICGtesting.com
Printed in the USA
BVHW011127161220
595607BV00019B/829